A R R I V A L   P R E S S

POETIC FINESSE

Edited by

TIM SHARP

First published in Great Britain in 1997 by
ARRIVAL PRESS
1-2 Wainman Road, Woodston,
Peterborough, PE2 7BU
Telephone (01733) 230762

All Rights Reserved

Copyright Contributors 1997

HB ISBN 1 85786 573 1
SB ISBN 1 85786 568 5

FOREWORD

The poets that are included in *Poetic Finesse* come from all walks of life; housewives and bank managers sit alongside council members and parents.

This anthology contains a selection of verse on every subject from remembrance to family values and from the environment to nature. The selected poems cover these areas and many more. This is a book you will enjoy reading again and again.

I hope you enjoy reading this book as much as I did whilst editing it.

Tim Sharp
Editor

CONTENTS

War Is Hell	NY Orks	1
Full Moon	W H Saunders	3
Water Skiing	Cathy Ann Legg	4
Home Coming	K E Brooker	5
As It Is	M W Brown	6
New Moves	Margaret Carter	7
What If?	Stacey McGill	8
Perfect Love	Audrey Evans	9
The Nineties - A Survey	Michael Jawornyj	10
Mother And I	Morgan Wilks	11
Eurostars	Graham Ronald Bell	12
Nineties Life In General	Mary Armstrong	13
Stop Smoking	Kathy Brown	14
Robots	J M James	15
My New Millennium	F Oldfield	16
The Fortunes Of Nature	Jill M Ronald	17
Absent Friends	Sandra D Dolman	18
Awakening	Sandy Parkes	19
To Whoever It May Concern	Louise King	20
The Beauty Around Us	Gill Sanbrooke	21
The Tree Of Friendship	Suzanne Firth	22
A Lover's Lament	F Coxhead	23
Irish Blood	Shaun Richard Hutton	24
Harm	Emma Garcia	25
The Carp	P J Williams	26
Changing Destiny	George A Naykene	27
The Blue Of The Sky	Leah Skinner	28
Bewitched	Malcolm Cowden	29
Have I Been Here Before	Dawn R Keeble	30
Who Am I?	A Robin Addey	31
A Tranquil Start	Daniel T O'Neill	32
I Let You Hurt Me!	Susan Fish	33
A Special Morning	Gina Wright	34
Thoughts And Feelings	D Feltham	35
Desire	Janice Logan	36
Birthdays And Christmas	Barry Kendall	37

Train Of Thought	Charlotte Sinclair	38
Red Pepper Joe	John McCann	39
Picture Of A Friend	Helen Bernard	40
The Quiet One	Denise Bracey	41
The Old People's Club	Jean Mallett	42
Bears	Susan C Bullman	43
Dream	Mary Lou	44
Lost Friends	S Durie	45
One For The Road	Ann Anderson	46
I Thought I'd Be A Hero	Marc Dermott	47
Critturs	Vera Markham	48
Hollow Hall	Ailin O Broin	49
In The Eyes Of A Child	Muriel Pearce	50
For You	J E Morgan	51
The Homecoming	Jenny Bosworth	52
Ocean Inamorata	Nina Denning	53
Stormy Night	Olive Irwin	54
Our Beautiful Earth	Julia Brigden	55
Unsung Heroes	Ann Odger	56
An Angel Of Mercy	Nannette Raybould	57
Exposers	Irene-Ann Fraser	58
Holiday Romance	Claire Chilton	59
Light To Exit By	David Charles	60
Old Father Thames	William G Hackney	61
Weymouth	Jacquie Williams	62
Lunar Eclipse	C Mulrooney	63
My Beer On A Beer Mat	Keith L Powell	65
A Drunken Man	Rachel Rainey	66
Family	David Evans	68
Billie Lived	Teresa Louis	69
The Storm	Sophie Bucknall	70
Try It And See	K F Foss	71
Waterwheels	Peter M Geary	72
Mysterious Place	Russell A Wells	73
Memories	L Johannes	75
Love	Maria Tangen	77
Potty Training Perfected!	Sally Sandever	78

Never Knowing, Always Regretting My Ways!	Rebecca Jones	79
	Tony Parkinson	80
Insight	R Abdul-Aziz	81
Remembrance Day 1996	Gwen Liddy	82
A Day In 1941	Lorna A McNeil	83
Brothers In War 1939/45	Len Beddow	84
Cornfields	Yona Geddes	85
A Candle	Kerry Nugent	86
D-Day 1994	Dennis Hawes	87
Child	Julie Hunt	88
Drugs	John Taylor	89
My Regrets	Lucy Jude	90
Love	Doreen Petherick Cox	91
Rules Of Engagement	Rebecca Summers	92
Millennium	Alison Clifton	93
Me And My Dog	Elizabeth McFarlane	94
Stage Fright	Diane Nunnerley	95
Taking Stock	Patricia Bibby	96
A Mother's Loss	N D Handley	97
The Boy	Gordon Lott	98
Forgotten Grandfather	Stuart Saw	99
Time	Lilian Bernard Levi	100
Hallowed Ground	Dorothy Thornley	101
Capital Punishment	Sarah Deacon	102
A Winter's Day	Suzanna Culshaw	103
The Fox	Christine Cocken	104
Gone At Last	Laila Street	105
Those Men (BEF 1940)	Fred Foster	106
London Blitz (1940-41)	Francis Sawyer	108
A Day To Remember	Cyril Rand	109
The Elysian Fields	Elisabeth James	111
A Nice Cup Of Tea	Aubrey Henstock	112
Somme And On	Peter James Warr	113
Shadows	Barbara Moore	114
Arthur	Jenny Ambrose	115
Sailor	Valerie Marshall	116
The Gulf War	Nola B Small	117

Remembrance Sunday	Lynda Banks	118
One Of The Few	Marianne G Sutherland	119
Charlie	Pip 'C'	120
Requiem	Arthur Pugh	121
The Forgiving Field	Roy Williams	122
Our Finest Hour	Lionel Reid	123
Pipe Dreams	Daf Richards	124
Counting The Cost	Robert A Plummer	125
Ghosts Of Nineteen Forty	Henry J Green	126
Stolen Youth	David Galvin	127
The Highwayman	Michele Glazer	128

War Is Hell

The first siren sounded on Sunday,
a day I still remember.
Yet life seemed the same on Monday.
I was seventeen, that September.

At first, most nights were tinged with fear,
awaiting the bombers onslaught,
Christmas came, and New Year,
to date our fears had come to nought.

Later that year I answered the call,
caught a train to RAF Padgate.
Few of us thought we were going to a ball
but some realised it too late.

A bigger fright than the declaration of war
came on first entering a Barrack Block,
all the signs of spit and polish we saw
left most of us in a state of shock.

The Stove surrounds were painted white,
bedside lockers, wooden, scrubbed.
Even the coal bunkers were polished bright.
There was nothing that didn't look rubbed.

The Lino, brown, looked like glass,
not a footprint anywhere,
anybody who that way had to pass
must have floated on air.

In the centre of the room stood the SGT/DISCIP.
HE was brushed and polished as well,
when he spoke it was like a crack of a whip,
He'd surely risen from hell.

'Take a look' he said 'and take note my boys
at the mop, polish and duster
You'll learn they are not just toys,
Cos you'll use them until you pass muster.'

'Reveille's at six, breakfast at seven, but before you take a bite,
this is how the room has to look, or you'll do it again at night,
till I say it's right.'

There's a list on the wall, find your name,
alongside it is stated your chore
each day you can win trouble or fame
cleaning walls, windows, or floor.

Of all the jobs, the one I got?
Not polishing floors or cleaning glass,
nor blackening up a stove still hot
from scrubbing, too, I got a pass.

Of all the chores, I'd got the best
Merely two pails to clean.
While they're all working I can rest
How very lucky I'd been.

On the first morning I watched them all sweat,
made no effort to hide my glee.
I sat back and smoked, couldn't start yet,
How they all envied me.

Then came the time to go and dine
on porridge, bacon and eggs.
But I couldn't yet go and get mine,
Two pails were still full of dregs.

NY Orks

FULL MOON

Full moon why do thou wear a troubled face
This night so bright and full of grace
The air so quiet . . . save for the breeze
The rustle of the branches in the trees.

O moon surrounded by a starry sky
Whose pale full face looks sad up there on high,
What can it be that makes you frown so deep?
While all the world is still . . . and most asleep.

Is it that you look upon a world
Of haunted minds and troubled hearts . . . which seek
A Utopia free from war . . . where all is peace
Not slaughter, massacre, sabotage, defeat?

O moon how envious all should be
Of you alone on high in heavenly peace.
Were all to be as thou . . . A Holy See,
The world would ever be . . . a land of peace.

W H Saunders

WATER SKIING

As I started to tremble in my skis,
The tall guy shouts it's your turn,
Carefully I waded through the glittering pure water,
As a shivering squirm descended down my back.

The cold ocean surf congregates around my body,
I glimpse at the boat as it slowly starts the roaring engine,
The fluorescent cord creaks as it's pulled tighter,
A warm glow lightens inside me.

'Three, two, one, hit it!' shouts the guy,
The cord straightened as it stretched, I started to glide slow,
The speed accelerates,
As the icy spray made me gasp with astonishment.

The feeling of euphoria swept over me,
It was over,
As the engine wound down,
I slid into the depths of the water.

Cathy Ann Legg

HOME COMING

When I come home from work on Fridays
    with toys and sweets for my children
I look upon the joy and happiness.
    showing on their faces.
The whole place becomes alive with rays of light
    dancing in the gloom.
With laughter echoing in darkened places,
    with cries of Daddy, Daddy here comes Daddy.
They open their sweet bags
    and look to see what toys they'd got.
The atmosphere becomes alive with joy.
What more can I ask, but to let them have their childhood,
They must not join us. Just yet.
    In hate and despair, not yet.
Let them stay young, and have their toys,
    and lots of fun.
Let their happiness, make all our sorrows,
    worthwhile.
A million lonely hearts would be cheered.
    to hear one sound of that laughter.
I could not give this up for riches or greed
    or any materialistic things
Let me remain a pauper, and yet own
    a million tears of happiness!

K E Brooker

As It Is

Who are we,
Born to strife and pain,
Unable to see life as a fleeting thought,
Between the planting and the growth,
Through the earthly seasons of sun and rain.

Born of a universe,
Where all things are contained,
In ordered confusion and time is myth -
Eternity reality that we cannot comprehend,
Because fear of the unknown still remains.

Not with possessions,
Or hoarding of wealth,
The power to debase others, and satisfy ourselves,
Not with the roar and blast of machines,
Which reach into space other worlds to explore.

The answer is simple,
And deep in our spirit,
Just a small particle this humanity,
Part of all nature on this planet called Earth -
Part of the whole, of God's vast infinity.

M W Brown

NEW MOVES

New Year, new start, new house for us
After 26 years, we will not fuss
Just pack our possessions and move on
Now that children have grown and gone.
Happy memories we made there
Love in a family, kindness and care
Improvements done, green trees were sown,
Extended garage - we got a loan.
Garden paths laid neat and clean
Then a nicer house was seen
Had we the courage to *get up and go?*
Advice was given it's great, and so
We are emptying boxes, and doing our best,
A warm cup of tea, now, time for a rest!

Margaret Carter

WHAT IF?

Last night while I lay thinking here
Some *what ifs* crawled inside my ear
　and pranced and partied all night long
And sang their same old *what if* song . . .

What if I fall on the way to school
What if I forget my gym kit
What if I am late for school
What if I don't pack my lunch
What if I fail my test
What if I lose my books
What if my hair smells of jam
What if I grow the size of the school
What if I shrink to the size of a mouse
What if I get bullied . . .

Everything seems swell and then . . .
The night time what ifs strike again . . .

Stacey McGill (10)

PERFECT LOVE

You've met someone special
Isn't life great,
You are really sure
he is your soul mate.

He is loving and warm
Swept you off your feet,
Yes you sigh
we were fated to meet.

But just stop and think,
when he's kissing you,
does he always ask
for a pound or two?

And when he tells you
You are *the one*
does he borrow your car keys
and then he's gone?

When you've just made love
and your passion is spent,
does he hint to move in,
there will be no rent!

This man is not for you
he'll certainly ruin your life
believe me, I know it's true
because I am *his wife!*

Audrey Evans

THE NINETIES - A SURVEY

A karaoke night at the Malt Inn -
And Sharon wins first prize with Jive Talkin'.
A new Beatles song on Top Of The Pops,
As the Sex Pistols re-form. New album in shops.
The Buddy Holly Story - a West End sellout,
And now the musical Grease is out and about.

Mini-skirts are once more fashionable,
Flared jeans and bell bottoms are no longer questionable.
Charity shops do a roaring trade in tank tops,
And it's welcome back to ankle socks.
Hair and beauty salons have a full book -
As women go for that Eva Peron look.

Daytime TV is showing us Payton Place,
And was that Starsky and Hutch in a car chase?
Crossroads is being repeated,
As the Carry On film season keeps us seated.
Alf Garnett calls his wife a silly moo,
And yet another programme on the 1966 World Cup Final on BBC2.

Dad renews his membership of the Volkswagen Beetle Club,
And mum wants a cast iron bath tub.
A 1968 Matchbox limited edition car would make Mark's day.
A Sindy doll please? - Asks young Rae.
Myself - I can't complain -
The corner shop is selling Spangle sweets once again!

Michael Jawornyj

MOTHER AND I

Mother is the plant
I am the seed,
The one she will love,
The one she will feed.
The one she will guide
Through thick and through thin,
For she is the fish
And I am the fin.

Mother is the word,
I am the letter.
Her guidance in life
Makes me better and better.
Thank you, dear Mum,
For all you have done.
You are the sky
And I am the sun.

Morgan Wilks

EUROSTARS

Panic on the Chunnel today.
Woke up to a bitter wind,
Scraping and scratching for visibility,
Wiping the glass to prepare a fresh
Battle ground for the war with condensation.

Straining on the roads, treading the pedals with
The delicacy of Chopin.
A virtuoso performance
Marked, not with a standing ovation,
But with a safe return.

Fire on the Chunnel.
Can ice penetrate 13 miles in?
Scraping and scratching
Of men's nails on courtesy car doors.
Breathing with the control of a concert tenor
To preserve the precious invisible.

Bravo! Escape.

Graham Ronald Bell

NINETIES LIFE IN GENERAL

Life in the nineties has been an education,
If not always, an inspiration
The sixties gave us, rock and fun
The fifties was when, I found life, in the sun.

The nineties has given us, some good group singers
Gentle soft words, from some beginners
Many made it, to the top
Some not there long, before the flop.

Some I was told, could really sing
But at my age, it sounded, like a din
The nineties has given us lots, of sport
Rugby, soccer and the tennis court.

More opportunities, to the disabled, the nineties, gave
At last, the girls could really rave
About the Adonis in the wheelchair
On equal terms, with the leg men there.

The nineties has, had tragedy and brains
Conquered pain, wars, and discovery, kept pride in reins
The Indian summer weather, not often seen before
Has brought beauty and pleasure, to each humble door.

The nineties has shown politics and scheming
Belongs in a world, of downfall and dreaming
We can go to Paris, without a ferry
Being a European, often causes worry.

It would be nice to have friends, all over the world
Before into the year, two thousand, we're hurled
So come from the east, and USA, visit our beaches, and be brave
We're British, and the nineties, we can't neglect, the tourist trade.

Mary Armstrong

STOP SMOKING

My aim this year is to kick to habit
Once and for all I'm going to stop it
I've tried before to no avail
Everytime I always fail
This time I mean it once and for all
If I stop I can walk tall
But it's not so easy on 20 a day
Even if it's a lot to pay
Here I am 3 hours gone by
Oh for a fag I do sigh.
Biting my nails and getting nasty
To hell with it pass me the ashtray
I'll have one today and stop tomorrow
I have no will power, to my sorrow
Just had a puff on my little fag
Feel much better after my drag.
I've cut down to ten aren't I good
Down to five I know I should
Hubby says pass down the fan
Be strong he says I know you can.
Sorry to say if I'm honest
I'm not one to break a promise
Don't think I'll ever stop
Unless they're banned from the shop.

Kathy Brown

ROBOTS

What do I think of the nineties,
  What I foresee not a lot.
We are becoming too automated,
  Our way of life will soon be forgot.
More we are using computers,
  For business, and in a game.
For questions use mouse, push a button,
  For an answer you don't need the brain
To shop we will look at the telly,
  To work we will use the lap top.
Soon no more need to go out,
  Meet with people, that will all stop.
No more need to travel for holidays,
  Put Virtual Reality that thing on your head.
That will pick your holiday for you,
  You just plug yourself in instead.

J M James

MY NEW MILLENNIUM

instead of sixty make it double
  easy done not much trouble
  in my new millennium text

doubling minutes that comes next
  hours and days follow suit
  weeks and months same to boot

  twenty four months in the year
  hang on a minute i'm getting there
    six months work in my new time
    equals twelve months work ain't that fine
six months rest what a joy
  everybody full employ

F Oldfield

THE FORTUNES OF NATURE

The New Year dawns in bitter cold,
The icy morning blast,
I wonder who would be so bold,
To forecast - will it last!

However, days grow longer hour by hour,
Trees about to bud,
The bulbs and blossom start to flower,
The cows chew on the cud.

Spring is with us once again,
As the birds begin to sing,
Animals frolic in the lane,
That same familiar ring!

The birds have nested here and there,
The blossom blown away,
No more time to stand and stare,
The grass to mow each day!

Summer-time has come once more,
With nature - oh so green!
The flowers as never seen before,
Such a show have been!

The sun begins to lose its heat,
The grass now is quite brown,
The world grows mellow and so sweet,
Although has lost its crown.

This time we've moved into the fall,
All orange, brown and red,
A sight that only can enthral,
Albeit nearly dead.

Jill M Ronald

ABSENT FRIENDS

The little girl with the round face,
the smile, her friendship a keepsake
we were like twins born together
to share God's land.
You went away and left me the
cross to bear.
You met new friends who held your
hands and share
I met up with you some years later
when I was wiser, but the love had gone
you weren't there.
I hoped we could rekindle the love
we shared but God took you away
suddenly with no time to spare.
Today I think of you and shed a tear
for the love we had was so dear.

Sandra D Dolman

AWAKENING

Locked in her own destiny,
With the fluttering of a living heart,
Somehow more alive.
This handsome stranger,
A friend for many years,
Leans forward
And with all the delicate sensation
Of a thousand heaven bound butterflies,
Kisses her.
This momentary collision of souls
Echoing into the future.
Two lives entwined,
One fate sealed.

Sandy Parkes

TO WHOEVER IT MAY CONCERN

I'm me
I'm independent, free, individual
I'm me
and I don't need you to crush me down
I'm myself
I'm different, creative, alive
I'm myself
and I don't see why I should be put down by you

Louise King

THE BEAUTY AROUND US

Think of the rose tinted dawn of day,
And a cooling shower of rain like teardrops falling fast,
Think of the flowers which have faded away,
Like so many dreams which did not last.

Think of the frosty night,
When a thousand diamonds on black velvet shine,
Look at the sun's brilliant light,
Warming the grapes to make a full-bodied wine.

Listen to a quietly murmuring stream,
Or a stormy, wind-lashed sea,
Think of a falling snowflake's gleam,
Or the beauty of a knarled old tree.

A cave is a thing of mystery to see,
And what is lovelier than a lone bird warbling in the rain,
Or a scarlet leaf blowing free,
As through the stillness church bells ring again.

Watch the leaves of burnished gold,
Ready to fall at autumn time,
Think of snow so white and cold,
Amid the joy of Christmas time.

Imagine a feather's gentle feel,
Or see the colours of a rainbow overhead,
Watch a bluebell's silent peal,
Or the sun sinking amid brilliant shades of red.

Think of the moon's silver beam,
And the summer breeze like laughter through the trees,
Think of you and think of me,
And how good our life together has been.

Gill Sanbrooke

THE TREE OF FRIENDSHIP
(This poem is dedicated to a very special friend, Helaina)

We sat like roots listening to the story of life,
A strong friendship was established,
A bond which through trust grew into a tree.
You told me of your dark and unforgettable past,
I heard cries, of pain, of anger,
And yet, knew not how you felt.
The branches grew thin and brittle.
The only strength was now in our friendship,
As we climbed the tree of life.
Although in the past branches had broken,
The tree kept on growing,
Providing the hope to keep on going.
The main body of the tree became history,
As I convinced you there was light at the end of the tunnel,
Our friendship became the statue to follow.
Because you'd been there, done that,
and nothing would go wrong again.
But still as the wind whistled through the tree,
The shadow of your past still lingered,
and the only solution was now time,
trust, and hope.

Suzanne Firth

A Lover's Lament

She moves gracefully like a breath of spring

Bright, fresh and pretty as a flower

So alluring, in her charms, past believing

So great they increase by the hour.

Old men, affected, they feel years fall away

Young men hope, and can only pray

Surely, such beauty is part of creation

Mortal though she is, yet heavenly she

For so she is to you and me.

F Coxhead

IRISH BLOOD

Pistol to head.
Knuckles white.
Fingers tight.
Trigger pulled.
Bullet sped.
Hole in head.
Pool of blood.

No compassion from eyes in hood.

Empty space, vacant air,
where a young man stood.

Catholic or Protestant:
it's Irish blood.

Shaun Richard Hutton

HARM

Saturday night and the party's wild,
Sophie's having fun,
Not knowing of the evening's laugh,
Or anything they'd done.

She was having fun enough that night
And didn't need a high
Someone spiked her drink you see,
What they'd told her was a lie.

A sip was all it took Sophie,
To pull her to the floor,
Everybody stood around,
One boy jumped for the door.

He was the guilty party
The one who'd spiked her drink
The effects to her were drastic
How low can someone sink?

The paramedics rushing,
They laid her on a bed,
They sped her to a hospital,
If only the truth was said.

He'd told her that he'd topped it up
With more lager, lime and ice
No-body feels the same as she
Who did then pay the price.

Emma Garcia

THE CARP

The summer morning was still and warm,
The water glistened after the night's storm.
The carp lay resting under the shade of the tree,
But ever watchful, so cunning was he.
Which made him a very difficult prey
For the angler to catch on this warm summer's day.
But hunger at last brought the big carp out
Into the lake he started to scout.
The fisherman watched, his tackle was ready,
His body was taut but his hand held steady
The rod with which he was to play
The fish down there feeding on this warm summer's day.
The bread on the water lay enticingly there,
And the carp rose up by it and gave it a stare,
But passed by it slowly ignoring the bread,
The angler's heart lurched and he lifted his head
To the heavens above he said a quick prayer,
And when he looked back the fish was still there.
The carp turned slowly with mouth opened wide
He sucked in the bread with the hook inside.
Too late he realised what he had done,
With the reel screeching loudly he made a run,
His only thought was somewhere to hide,
He reached the weeds and dashed inside.
He felt the hook that tore at his lip,
And angrily he gave a flip.
With tail upturned he stood on his snout,
And as the line loosened the hook fell out.
Back under the tree he went to lie low,
Once more the prey had beaten his foe.
The angler packed up and went on his way,
The carp lay basking, happy, on this warm summer's day.

P J Williams

CHANGING DESTINY

Oh! How can I change my destiny
  Who can help me change my destiny.
For I was a child born in sorrow.
  Even my name connotes sorrow

My mother named me sorrow because I was
  born under unfavourable and unpleasant circumstances
My mother had me out of holy wedlock, and my father
  Could not be identified, thus causing my mother
a lot of embarrassment and concern

My name follows me throughout my life
  but thanks to the almighty I have made it
through a child of sorrow I have changed
  my condition by praying in faith.

My brother you can also change your destiny
  through faith in the name of the Lord Jesus Christ.
For faith is the substance of living hope for
  and the evidence of things not seen. Amen

George A Naykene

THE BLUE OF THE SKY

How wonderful to see
a garden full of blue;
bluebells, forget-me-nots,
pansies and aubretia.
When the sun shines on a mass
of blue petals,
a blue haze hovers,
mist-like, in the air.

No other colour has this effect.
I wonder why?
Is it because they reflect
the blue of the sky?

Leah Skinner

BEWITCHED

You came to me so late last night
As I lay sweetly sleeping
Silently as dawning light
Was through my curtain peeping

I wakened as you touched my face
And held me with your eyes
No loving me with fond embrace
No cheating words or lies

I wonder where you were last night
Whose company you were keeping
And why you came to me at light
As I was gently sleeping

I know that other men than me
Have fallen for your charms
That Mr Brown at number three
Has held you in his arms

I hope that you enjoyed the meal
He made for you that day
And understand you made me feel
So pleased you didn't stay

Although to me you've been untrue
And perhaps you've been unwise
But you know I'll always love you
When you hold me with your eyes

You're welcome now once more to roam
I know you can't help that
Rejoicing when you come back home
To be once more my cat.

Malcolm Cowden

HAVE I BEEN HERE BEFORE

How many lifetimes have I lived before,
who was I, when, and where?
How can I explain these feelings
of being here once or twice before?
Was I black, or was I white or maybe
somewhere in between?
What must I learn this time around
that maybe I did not then?
Was I a woman like 'Joan of Arc',
burnt in front of people at the stake?
Or was I a man on the battlefield
with sword and shield fighting human race?
Was I a queen who with her king
sat on the royal throne by him?
Or was I a mother, who sat with her lover
rocking the cradle the baby lay in?
Whatever I was with the De-Ja-Vu
that I've been here before.
I know this time I must get it right
so I can come back to learn some more.

Dawn R Keeble

WHO AM I?
(Dedicated to Rachel)

I like sweets
And chocolates too
Given the chance
I eat quite a few.

I'm super of course
(Though I say it myself!)
At waiting at tables
So why help yourself?

Come try me out
I'm second to none
In a matter of seconds
Serve tea and a bun!

A bill I'll prepare
- But charge you double
If you go to the Nutmeg
Or cause me trouble!

A Robin Addey

A Tranquil Start

So blue was the sky today
that the moon had failed its head to lay
A gentle breeze in the early morn
accompanied the feathered morning song

True strength of the moon's dear kin
had not yet begun to sing
Unlike those of the flighted choir will do
that collect and dine of morning's dew

The morning's peace and tranquil will ease
to give way to the sun's new piece
Until then I'll enjoy the day's prime glisten
and look forward to the next beginning

Daniel T O'Neill

I Let You Hurt Me!

For all the hurt you put me through,
throughout the years I spent with you,
How I must of been so blind,
I ignored everyone's advice on how
you would never treat me right and nice
After the years of endless pain
I let you hurt me yet once again.
Sitting night after night you ignored the tears I cried,
I tried and tried for us, I tried to love you once again
But again I let you break my heart
There is only one thing that I can thank you for
Is our little boy I love and adore.
Now I'm alone, you're with someone else
and now I hate you even more
Now I've woken to reality, you were never the man
for me,
I only wish I'd realised, how so blind I must of been.

Susan Fish

A Special Morning

Oh how I love your letters,
Such a quiet way to chat,
We can often put the world to right
Exchanging notes on this and that.

I know the telephone is handy
And it's nice to hear the spoken word,
But when we have a lot to say
The bill becomes absurd.

A little stamp is almost nothing
And it pays for many a mile,
And just writing on an envelope
Can create an instant smile.

What has the postman brought me
Is that another bill I see?
Well I'll just leave it on the floor
And make a cup of tea.

But wait a flipping minute
Just hang on a mo'
There's an envelope with proper writing
In a friendly hand I know.

So let's put on the kettle
And make a lovely brew,
For this is a *special morning*
I've got a letter from you.

Gina Wright

THOUGHTS AND FEELINGS

Why have we no time to stand and see
The wonders all around
A rippling stream, a new born lamb,
Spring flowers on the ground

In a hurry we all seem to be
Day in day out the same old grind
Worried, frustrated, full of woe
All seem to have no peace of mind

Material things seem to be
The most important things today
Get this, get that we have it now
Is all people seem to say

But are these things so very good
For one's own peace of mind
If people only looked around
For better things they'd find

D Feltham

DESIRE

Desire!

A powerful word, an overwhelming emotion.

For the man or woman who find themselves desiring another.
Shall lose the power to reason.
As in those moments of desire, time stands still, frozen and locked.
All other commitments banished and easily forgotten.

The desired shall reason not, allowing themselves to be intoxicated and enticed.
Simply bask in the admiration.
Whilst they gaze upon this face alight with the joy of them.
And cannot deny the pleasure of it.

To acknowledge and rejoice in another's need to be with you.
Touch you.
Lie with you.
Stroke and caress you.
Know the physical and mental torment in the pulsating ache to have you.
Body, mind and soul.
There can be no mistaking the thrill of it.

For those who know they are desired.
Whether it be for a lifetime or even the briefest moment.
Shall feel fulfilled.

Janice Logan

BIRTHDAYS AND CHRISTMAS

I've come around every day to see you,
I've been doing it for many a year.
I've come on your husband's birthday,
and up on the wall is a card,
to dad happy birthday from your son.
This card should be meant for me,
but our son he does not know you know.

Christmas comes around,
I am there again at your invitation.
On the wall a card for all to see,
to mum and dad from your son at Christmas.
The dad should be me.
Our son he does not know you know,
but no feelings do you show.

Barry Kendall

TRAIN OF THOUGHT

From dark to light,
From dull to bright
My life goes round
From touch to sound,
From smell to taste
Less speed, more haste
Travels on travel up
Through bad and good luck
Like wheels on a train
Through sun, snow and rain
My life carries on
Through love and pain
Meets people meets hearts
It stops and starts
It's found a station
It's going to stay in
The heart of a boy
Who brings love and joy,
It travels no longer
As the love grows stronger
No need to move on
As it's found the one.

Charlotte Sinclair

RED PEPPER JOE

Red Pepper Joe was a tiny wee mouse,
Who lived in the wall, of a great mansion house.
He lived like a king, with velvet and silk,
Dined on rich cheese, and the finest of milk.
His first love was Sarah, so pretty and fair,
Emerald green eyes and mousy brown hair
They married one day, in the middle of June,
And sat holding hands, under the palest blue moon.

John McCann

PICTURE OF A FRIEND

A friendly smile
A helping hand
No charge for her advice
She is a friend
A friend who's nice
One in a million
A heart of gold
Secrets are kept
They won't be told
Full of kindness to the end
Over backwards she will bend
This is the picture of a friend.

Helen Bernard

THE QUIET ONE

It has touched our lives with sorrow.
Some will never see their tomorrow,
Others will still close their eyes,
Not caring who lives or who dies.

We must care for who it will touch,
That's all we ask it's not much,
Dig deep into your well filled banks,
So the victims and families can give thanks.

To all the people who try hard to find,
A cure for AIDS and all of its kind,
We thank you from our very hearts,
The children will at least have a start.

One day they will find a cure,
And our families will be safe, I'm sure,
Until then give and understand their plight,
'Cos it could hit you or yours, maybe tonight!

Denise Bracey

THE OLD PEOPLE'S CLUB

How old is she, they ask, and have you seen her dress?
I wonder what her husband's like and where is her address?
The woman they're discussing is all of eighty-five.
From the outside you might well wonder: is she still alive?

But under the besilvered hair and within the wrinkled skin
She keeps a secret hidden of which they're not aware.
Where did all the years go? What happened to the time?
How long ago the wars seem! Is old age such a crime?

She still loves brilliant colours and having her hair done.
She still would love to dance - it really was such fun.
The man that she did marry was once so brave and tall,
And now he stoops and wanders as if not there at all.

The children that she carried as the produce of her love
Have long since all been married, have children of their own.
Those children have their children, and if they think of her at all
It's as a relic of the past, from a time way past recall.

Yet where did all the time go? What happened to her life?
When did she forsake her teens? What happened to the love?
'Inside me, I am seventeen,' she longed to shout out loud,
But still they helped, put out a chair, assumed she needed it.

They didn't look like seventeen. They looked so old, she thought.
Poor things, she muttered to herself, perhaps they should be told?
So the lady stood and shouted loud, 'I'm only seventeen, you know.'
And the rest - well they just looked and said, 'She's ill, you see.'

Jean Mallett

BEARS

Everyone loves teddy bears
Cuddly cute with glassy stares
Furry soft, find comfort there
Lined on the window sill
And sat upon the bed they grace
Filled with foam and sweet of face
We take them to our side
Yet behind that jolly friendly face
From faraway gazes back a sadder face
Of dancing bears trained in sad torment
No sign of fun or merriment
As they dance round and round
Taken from the wild their pride
Caged no room to turn inside
Chains embedded in their skin
Holding freedom cruelly from them
For living bears in real coats of fur
No comfort for them anywhere
Why do we all care so much
For objects that cannot feel our touch
When there is so much distress and dispair
For the real teddy bear . . .

Susan C Bullman

DREAM
(For Harvey)

You're like a dream
You come and go . . .
I walk in a trance,
Starlight . . . glow.

You fill me with love
Sublime and serene . . .
You come and go . . .
You're like a dream.

Mary Lou

LOST FRIENDS

How many friends have come and gone
and gone and gone
over the years, so many lost
somewhere in the wastes of life.

Where are they now, I wonder,
at the mid-point of my life
All those people claiming friendship
And vanished, it seems, forever.

Oh I'm so busy
Seems to be the usual cry:
Which I think I will adopt
As my recurring refrain.

However, I know those who are
never so busy, never vanish:
who remain constant
and constantly beside me -
My little cats,
abandoned, dumped and deserted
by others:
My shadows and companions
Forever.

S Durie

ONE FOR THE ROAD

Two minutes to spare
How best to spend
Do you drive at top speed
Overtake on a bend.
Will it live in your memory
The ambulance ride
They tell you you're lucky
But you're dying inside
For the sake of two minutes
One over the few
A man's death on your conscience
Who's lucky
        not you.

Ann Anderson

I Thought I'd Be A Hero

I thought I'd be a hero
When I left my home that day
For I knew to be a soldier
I would have to run away

Then I put on my uniform
And polished my boots with pride
Standing to attention
With my rifle at my side

We sailed across the channel
Dug the trenches one by one
And everyone was confident
By Christmas we'd be home

But excitement turned to horror
And courage into fears
Moral was slowly fading
And the months turned into years

The battle raged, the bullets flew
The fight went on and on
The wounding and the bloodshed
Until at last the war was won

But now as I remember
When we fought side by side
I knew who were the heroes
The brave men who had died

Marc Dermott (13)

CRITTURS

Roll back the edges of the lawn,
Below the garden wall.
There they live; in their damp
Gloomy land,
'Critturs' one and all.

Strange looking crawlers on strange
Legs,
Dozens of spiders. Nowhere to go . . .
This is their territory; in rain or in
    snow.

I see a big cluster of baby snails;
So small, that you cannot believe
That mama snail knows they really
    exist.
But soon they'll grow and crawl.

It's a place of wonder for a five year old.
As she pokes and prods and exclaims,
'I think that these 'critturs' are happy,
on the day that it rains!'

Vera Markham

HOLLOW HALL

Standing tall,
like the fairy queen above her domain,
your laughter tumbles down the stairs,
bounces along the hall walls,
tracing the path of your bouncing ball,
to fill the house with the air
of your child's happy refrain.

The bouncing ball,
leaping and dancing as it leaves your hands,
is the magic star flying from the wand
of Tinker Bell, weaving the path
of your mesmeric laugh,
fixing me where I stand,
as it flies into my waiting hands.

But the happy sound you bring
to this hollow hall
will follow you soon
on your journey away.
The silence that will stay
will pain us all.

How we will hate the quiet.
And if we hear your laugh
we will cry; for it is only
an echo of the happy days
you brought us before I gave you up -
before I gave you away.

Ailin O Broin

IN THE EYES OF A CHILD

So wonderful are the eyes of a child
No evil can they see
So innocent and beautiful
I wish they belonged to me.

So pure they are like angels' eyes
In the clear blue sky above
Oh how I wished I had that child's eyes
To see the things I love.

I once had the eyes of a child
I thought the world was great
I never knew when I grew up
It would be so full of hate

I used to watch the flowers
Blooming in the spring
And then I'd watch the little birds
And they would start to sing.

Muriel Pearce

FOR YOU

The sunshine of spring I wish for you
The joy of a golden day
A playful breeze, a shower or two
And the sight of lambs at play
All these are part of God's own plan
The sunshine and the rain
We need them both to help us grow
To make us whole again.

J E Morgan

THE HOMECOMING

Someday,
Every once in a while.
We will pack a suitcase
And go off in style.

Somewhere,
Just up the road
A house or hotel
Will be our abode.

Someone,
Will look after you well
You get a suntan
And a few yarns to tell.

But somehow,
When the time we recall
We realise that coming home
Was the best part of all.

Jenny Bosworth

Ocean Inamorata

Alone by the sea
You and me
Passion warms the breeze
Softly, softly the ocean breathes

Here by the sea
Love enraptures me
Like the waves we fall
Eclipsed in moonlight's shawl

Alone by the sea
Flirting with destiny
Lost in a lover's abyss
We share a stolen kiss

Sands of sensuality
Set me free
Embrace my fears
Consume my lonely tears

Spirit of the salty sea
Stay with me
This pain inside is true
For I see his beauty in you

Alone by the sea
Seduced by memories

If only you knew
Of the ocean girl
Who fell in love with you.

Nina Denning

STORMY NIGHT

The rain and the wind
like a stormy tropical
romance, wild and free
Dancing through their
minds, beating of hearts
the sound of the wind
howling like a hungry
wild animal inside each
other, they lay in each
other's arms as the
storm begins again.

Olive Irwin

Our Beautiful Earth

When God created the earth, with forests and seas and sky,
He must have had a reason, and I think that I know why.
He wanted man to destroy it all as ruthlessly as he could.
We have surpassed ourselves, as God, you knew we would.

We've put up some concrete and smashed down some trees.
Just look God, we are trying hard to please.
We've polluted all the water, now we're working on the air.
It really is not difficult to do it everywhere.

We've thrown in some warfare, murder and greed.
And made sure there are too many mouths to feed.
We've introduced abortion to kill unwanted life.
And we've spread diseases that are now quite rife.

What's the matter God, why do you frown?
Because you must admit that we haven't let you down.
All the wondrous beauty of your creation.
Has now been destroyed by each and every nation.

Or have we got it wrong God, wasn't that your plan?
Your earth would still be beautiful, if it hadn't been for man.

Julia Brigden

UNSUNG HEROES

Dedicated to their calling
bound by the Hippocratic oath,
stitching cuts and wounds appalling
or treating an unsightly growth.
Knowing they are always needed
whatever time, by day or night,
patients asking to be heeded,
soothing our nerves when sick with fright.
Through sleepless night and hectic day
to always smile 'tho feeling rough,
expected to know just what to say,
sometimes wishing it was enough.
Wondering if we ever stop
to think they might be feeling low
often working until they drop,
rarely thanked for what they know.
Bedside manner and healing hand
to make the patient feel at ease,
hoping they will understand
good or bad news, we're hard to please.
No other work can be compared
so little outlet for emotion,
carry the thought we know they cared,
and be grateful for their devotion.

Ann Odger

AN ANGEL OF MERCY

Things got lost for a while
A lot I had to turn
Returning memories to my world
I am reborn again to learn.

Some things give me more pleasure
Along the road in life
I am on the road to recovery
So I will always be your wife.

Just as you like pool and football
My garden I love so
To dig and plant some seeds
Then wait for them to grow.

Then, when I cook our dinner
Some fruit or veg I need
I go into my garden
And pick from my planted seed.

Things got lost for a while
I really went down hill
Until I saw a surgeon
And got an operation, not a pill.

I am not a religious woman
But I've been reborn again to learn
I've been given a second chance at life
I'm going to grab it, it's my turn.

Thanks again one and all
It really is a delight
Except for all the drugs I had
The effects can give you a fright.

Nannette Raybould

EXPOSERS

If I try to be too cerebral;
It's then I stumble and fall;
Much preferring to come naturally;
Watching my pen flow freely;
Unfolding in front of my eyes;
Events, in everyday lives;
And it's just like within minutes;
I see it all down and finished;
It's then I know, this is inside;
A psychoanalysis, in black and white;
This pen's my problem sorter to me;
Believing in what I peruse and see;
Us lyricists expose just what we are;
We're constant watchers from afar.

Irene-Ann Fraser

HOLIDAY ROMANCE

We met at a bar,
And I believe I was pissed,
I was on holiday,
It was on the beach that we kissed.

You were a stranger in the night,
But I felt like taking a chance,
Wasn't the moon beautiful,
The scene set for romance?

We went to your room,
And my mind was in the skies,
But it wasn't until the next morning,
That I discovered all your lies.

What can I say,
I thought your love was true,
But it wasn't all that bad,
At least I never slept with you.

Claire Chilton

LIGHT TO EXIT BY

Through the longest darkest night,
Shines a beacon of hope to light your way
to guide you over the highest mountain
both by day and by night
not to whisper if only - but might
a symbol used over a thousand years
no words are needed - no need to fear
Secure - orange glow - off the candles' halo
- Let peace grow -

David Charles

OLD FATHER THAMES

Old Father Thames
Rolls down to the sea,
And I came to this river
In the year 'thirty three',
Long hours I worked
A mere lad of fourteen,
On board a barge
By name 'Essex Queen'
Our skipper we nicknamed
'Old Captain Bligh',
Ne'er a thing did he miss
with his steely blue eye.
When war clouds they gathered
I went far away
And I never returned for many a day.
Now sometimes in memory
I am young - fancy free,
On Old Father Thames
rolling down to the sea.

William G Hackney

WEYMOUTH

Crowds of people sit on the sand
my husband and I hand in hand
gaze out to sea, where ships are swaying,
Seagulls drifting, donkeys neighing,
Children's laughter echo on the breeze
candyfloss cotton, and busy bees
flurries of sand, sea so clear
joyful sounds from the pier,
A dreamy day where happiness surrounds
as the sunshine spreads her warmth around.
The waves of the sea
crash to the shore
as children run back
then run fore,
Some tea and a hot-dog
a deckchair to lounge
and listen to all the seaside sounds,
The call of the gulls and swell of the sea
my soul is at peace
as peace should be,
But too soon we embark on the journey home
sadness befalls
I wish we could roam
forever and always by the sea
where tranquillity and peace
will always be.

Jacquie Williams

LUNAR ECLIPSE

the muse compels
as of old
contemplation
up the tired avenue to
rangers and flares
parking and the smell of pines
the look of pines
and the desecrated Greek Theatre
then a slow bus ride a schoolbus
cramping the knees
back to Knott's Berry Farm
faces and lights rocks trees
lamps
roads and intersections other people

The Observatory's twin green breasts
a Planetarium atween
look down on two matching hillocks
afore the city
amateur telescopists have gathered
round the sacrosanct architecture

a small motionless group play ring around the
rosy
for hours then fall down in pairs
guitar nerds burble

a wee mouse emerges
from a hole in the concrete
by the head of James Dean
in bronze 20 Japanese girls
pose crouching beside
one by one to the last
giggling stragglers

at last the moon appears
out of the fog
a quarter blotted
by shadow

it is photographically clear
by telescope

we descend with a joyrider
at the wheel
to the vexful city

the moon emerges from
its last tip of shadow
into full
above the pine-trees and crickets
and lamps
and the streets

C Mulrooney

MY BEER ON A BEER MAT

I put my beer on a beer mat
To keep the table clean
It saves the bar person
From coming out of a dream.

I put my beer on a beer mat
So I know which one it is
For sometimes I get the wrong one
And drink one belonging to a miss.

I put my beer on a beer mat
Really late at night
For I too am really sleepy
And it won't escape from my sight.

Keith L Powell

A DRUNKEN MAN

I saw a drunken man on my walk
He lay on the corner of Saint Street
He did not speak but babbled in his talk
Like a stream that is only half awake.

I was silent with my anger
How could he be so drunk
In the middle of the day
Why do people behave in such a repulsive way?

I spoke but he knew no conversation
He fell; I quickly moved away,
Some young lad helped him to his feet
As blood poured down his cheek I heard him say

'My wife and family are all gone
Alone is no life for me,
What shall I do, where will I go?
Help an old man to be freed.'

'Freed of this old age and pain
In my heart for Mary, and shame
On me to my dying day -
When I left her and went my own way.'

Alone they left him hanging there
Propped up against a wall
Ragged and torn like a piece of clay
His suit all crumpled, old and grey.

My anger vanished as I saw his blood
And felt his angered pride,
How he longed to go back to his wife
To have her at his side.

When I tried to give him my hand
His pride made him push me aside,
And as his tears fell down his face,
My tears of sorrow I could not hide.

Finally an old mate came along,
Gave him his arm and led him home.
But the face of that man today
Shall stay with me always.

His blood I mixed with my tears today,
For pity now reigns supreme in my heart.
I can understand his shame and his pride,
He has no one to love him and nowhere to hide.

Rachel Rainey

FAMILY

My mum is on the bingo
My dad is on the booze
My sister's gone to town
and my brother is on the loose.
My gran is weird and wonderful,
My grandad is so funny!
He's just won ten pound
on the national lottery.

David Evans

BILLIE LIVED

Billie Billie if you could see
How you lived has effect on me
When did your world turn blue
Was it when they hounded you

That troubled spirit haunted voice
You stopped your fight did you have a choice
Was it the strange fruit beneath the sky
Or the dirt kicked in your eye.

If you was alive today
I'd encourage you to smile and pray
Your music lives it will never cease
I hope your soul is now at peace

Teresa Louis

The Storm

The trees are bending low today
The sky is wild the sky is grey
The river's rising fast and clear
The village flood fills me with fear
The horses neigh in stable yard
Around the house the wind blows hard
The hills are black and gaunt and bare
As I walk by with streaming hair.
I turn my steps toward my home
This is no time for me to roam.
Beside the fire I want to be
With my precious family.

Sophie Bucknall

TRY IT AND SEE

When you travel the underground,
It's pretty certain you'll be bound -
To look across the carriage space
Trying to miss the opposite face.
Upwards, downwards, left and right
Moving your eyes, just in case you might
just catch a glimpse of someone's stare
which really makes you more aware
that in this world, there's nothing new -
They are doing just the same as you.

K F Foss

WATERWHEELS

I'd taken on strange projects, but this one beat the lot,
Taking all the ingenuity I hoped to God I'd got,
Commissioned by a neighbour who has guts beyond her years,
I dared not brief my draughtsmen, I couldn't stand their jeers.

She'd been keen on ocean racing but now aged eighty three,
She's fed up with her wheelchair and wants to go to sea,
She heard that I'm an engineer, it was Tuesday she phoned me
She begged me not to laugh at her but I giggled fit to pee.

An outboard on her wheelchair was what she wanted most,
To go back out to sea again and sail from coast to coast,
I said I thought this madness, it would never ever work,
But I took it as a challenge, and my partner went berserk.

We designed it using fibreglass and also marine ply,
To float the chair on water and also keep it dry,
On the back we planned a Seagull with two horsepower or so,
And with no wind assistance some three knots she should go.

My client loved the drawings and praised our weird design,
She didn't want the Seagull but the rest she said was fine,
She'd need a Johnson forty for what she'd got in mind,
So her ninety year old husband could water-ski behind.

Peter M Geary

MYSTERIOUS PLACE

Under the lights
Where no shadows are cast
No one is first
And no one is last
From high upon high
To crevices deep
This mysterious place
Where death cannot reach
Where sky is not blue
And trees are not green
This place is on show
But it's never seen.

Where the air is so still
With the silence it makes
Where tormented hearts lie
Into pieces it breaks
Where cold it will boil
And heat it will freeze
This mysterious place
Will do what it please
In this dark dark place
That knows no pain
Nothing is lost
And nothing gained.

No entry, no exit
No need to know
With spells that are broken
Before they are sown
This place will hold you
For as long as it please
Before letting you go
On a cold silent breeze
It won't let you know
Just where you've been
Was this part of life
Or a mysterious dream

Russell A Wells

MEMORIES

The stars seem to shine
So brightly, and yet
They remind me of you.
The way you sparkled
When you smiled,
Your eyes filling with tears
As you laughed,
Yet it was all a disguise
Wasn't it?

But we all fell for it!
The pain and anguish
You hid inside, you hid so well.
You smiled and shrugged your shoulders
When life didn't go as planned,
Life's too short, you said
And just smiled.

Now that's all that's left
Our memories of you
And your smile.
And no one can ask
The questions that burn inside them.
For no answer can be found.
When you left, you took our world,
Our dreams and hopes.
You took all the answers and
Now we must struggle onwards
And be strong.
If not for us, then for you.

We will not forget you
For you will always remain
In our hearts.
And even though the sun will
Still rise and set the same and
Life will carry on, time won't
Be stopped, we will always love
You for who you really were.
We have our memories
And no one can destroy these.

L Johannes

LOVE

Love can mean so many things
To some it's good to others it's bad
Some people want it yet some people fear it
One minute you've got it, the next you've lost it
Will it come back or is it gone for good
Will it be the same or will it be new
No one knows until it comes to them
At one time or another it will come to us all
And when it does come just make sure it stays.

Maria Tangen

POTTY TRAINING PERFECTED!

I was sat in my nappy
When I realised I was wet.
It was time for toilet training
But I didn't have the equipment yet.
So off we went shopping
For a toilet seat and potty,
I duly 'performed' -
It was nice to air my botty.
My audience clapped and cheered
And I thought 'I've got the hang of it'
So I decided I'd do it myself
When I was alone for a bit.
I took my toilet seat to the bathroom
I knew what I had to do.
I took off my nappy
And then studied the loo.
The loo looked awfully high so
I put my seat on the floor,
'What a clever boy I am', I thought
As I left them a present by the door!

Sally Sandever

NEVER KNOWING, ALWAYS REGRETTING

I long for him to understand,
exactly how I feel,
I wish for once that I could say
- 'Yes, our love that's real.'

But deep down inside I know,
he'll always be someone I see,
but who'll never be for me.

I still hold a hope,
even when I cannot cope,
that maybe he feels the same,
although I guess he'll see it all as a game.

I dream of us being together,
I imagine us as forever,
yet I know we'll never be,
what I so desperately want to see.

I spend my life always regretting,
desperate to be forgetting,
but the problem is, I can't do all I dream,
as I never say what I really mean.
The doubt in me, won't let me try,
and when I stop myself, I can't help but cry.
If only I knew a way,
to make me say,
exactly what I feel,
then I could make my dreams become real.

So maybe all this wishing, one day may come true,
perhaps only then will I stop feeling blue.

Rebecca Jones

MY WAYS!

My frustration is to
understand my own destination
and all the situations
in my own life.

My disappointment I have
to see and know
the ultimate design
which I have to engage in.

My failure of expectation
I feel so well
arrive at the final result
to bind by contract.

Prospect of reaching
a certain age
a time that's to come
then become drawn together
forever in time.

My answers I find
become true for me
by the unknown
secrets of mystery.

Tony Parkinson

INSIGHT

You lie there, staring me in the face
your eyes searching mine.
I reach out to touch you,
and for a moment a connection is made.
This connection lasts only a few seconds
but it seems like an eternity.
And in that eternity I see a small
piece of your heart.

This heart is young and has so much to give and you grace me
with the knowledge of your years.
You show me your pain, anger, anxiety
and I feel that for a moment
I may have helped.

The connection is broken, and again
I see you lying there.
Your eyes are now full of tears
that acknowledge the relief of finally
opening your soul.
I feel honoured that you shared
with me something that I
will never forget.

R Abdul-Aziz

REMEMBRANCE DAY 1996

Overhead the sky is dark this day
Rain drops fall like angel tears from heaven
A distant gun booms across roof tops grey
And Big Ben tolls the hour of eleven.

The crowd around the Cenotaph stands
In silent prayer for the nation's dead
And like the cries of a million lost souls
A sighing breeze dries the tears they shed.

Ten thousand have assembled this special day
To march in memory of comrades who
Served their country and gave their lives
To achieve a victory they never knew.

Escorted by the young lions of today
Marching tall with confident stride
These veterans of conflicts long ago
Wear their medals with such pride.

As they pass let us be forever grateful
When the nation was almost on its knees
At the time of our mortal peril
We had such men as these.

But in applauding the living who march today
Let us not forget the reason they are here
And for the many dead we pray
And like heaven's angels shed a tear.

Gwen Liddy

A Day In 1941

Sitting at night
Listening to the radio.
Curtains pulled tight
No light to be seen.

Sirens start wailing
Dash towards the shelter.
Bombs start falling
Exploding too close for comfort.

Coming out the shelter
Relief at daylight.
Houses still standing
Everyone still alive.

Lorna A McNeil

BROTHERS IN WAR 1939/45

Eindhoven, Holland, just a town
A welcome awaited us there
And such a time! had we but known
Our speed would have been greater.

From the outskirts to the centre
Our progress was slow, crowds too dense
Flowers cover the tank, roses' scent
We must get through, every one tense.

Amidst clapping and cheering
CO's order, 'The war must wait
Out of your tanks,' we were hearing
To help the Dutch to celebrate.

Inside the nearest cafe, a table
Glasses of wine, jugs of beer
Helping himself, 'cause he was able
My brother, not seen for three year

More was to follow, there's my twin
Dancing with a pretty Dutch girl
Could see the kind of mood he's in
For he was giving her a twirl.

We painted the town a bright red
It had been a welcome break
Next morning, getting out of bed
We were all too tired to wake.

Len Beddow

CORNFIELDS

In the cornfields of England
Where the blood red poppies grow
The corn is ripe - the ears are full
T'will soon be time to mow.

There are fields in a far off land
Where blood red poppies grow
Fields where young men fought and died
In a land they did not know.

In other fields white crosses stand
Where once the corn grew tall
Thousands upon thousands sleep, the men
Who bravely gave their all.

Do you think they sleep contented?
Do you think they know?
They saved the English cornfields
Where the blood red poppies grow.

Yona Geddes

A Candle

A candle is lit I'm hot
I am dying
I am blown out
Oh no! I'm not dead?
I'm cold now
I am broken
I'm in the bin
Don't like it in here
All bits of candle
All what is left of me
Is bits of wax
And my wick has gone
Oh no! I'm getting crushed
I am dead.
Oh well I will get made into
Something.

Kerry Nugent (7)

D-DAY 1994

We stood in Bayeux cemetery among the service dead
While the prayers, the hymns and the lesson were read.
Gave thanks for long years of our deliverance
By the hand of God or by some mysterious chance.
Thought of the fallen, what they might have achieved,
Of their families, unborn children and silently grieved.
Pondering their courage, agony and final sacrifice,
Accepting that the defeat of evil was worth the price.
We felt some honour at sharing the historic D-Day battle,
The campaign, the trials and stinking dead cattle.
Then, before the Queen at Arromanches we paraded together,
The place we captured, despite ferocious foe and weather.
The Hampshires then led the parade with undisguised pride,
With shadows of their old comrades marching beside.

Dennis Hawes

CHILD

She stood there, silent by the door
A tiny child
Imprisoned by fear,
Trapped by her insecurity.
Many passed her by
Unaware of her pain.
Many more befriended her
Unaware of her need.

She locked away her fear, her pain, her needs
As she blossomed into womanhood,
Until she could hide them away no more.

But there came one whom she loved,
Who she could trust.
She wanted him to have her all,
So she cried to him,
Child by the door.
She cried for release, for her independence
And though she had cried before
This time she knew it was different,
He would come to her aid.

He came.
A shout of joy saw that tiny child
Run
Across the room
And fall into the arms of love.

Released
Into the everlasting arms
Where freedom reigns.

Julie Hunt

DRUGS

Drugs are stupid
they're deadly and dear
they blow out your brains
they make you disappear.

Ecstasy

People think they're 'ard
when they take this drug
but when they're lying ill in bed
they squirm like a little bug.

Heroin

The person who took this drug
is very very stupid,
he went down and met the Devil
and said 'I wish that I was Cupid.'

Coke

It's not Coke the drink
it's Coke the drug
that's what my friend died of
yes my friend Doug.

Pot

The safest drug to take
is pot, yes it is,
it is not as bad as the rest
but it's still a deadly kiss.

Don't take drugs!

John Taylor

MY REGRETS

You came along
With a smile for everyone.
You shared your laughter
and your chocolate.
You drove loud lorries.
I remember that, because that's how
you met my mum.
You moved in.
I resented that, I resented your presence
your laughter; your smile.
But they never went away.
You fought for my affection,
but I refused to acknowledge you.
You made everybody laugh
While I sulked and missed out.
You made my mum happy
but I wanted to do that.
You never backed down.
You hurt when I hurt.
You cried when I cried.
I spent all those years wishing you'd
go away.
And now you have,
And I miss you.
I know it's too late,
but I realise now,
Just what you had, and what you gave
And how hard you tried to make me love you.
And I know I never said it,
but for what it means,
I love you.

Lucy Jude

LOVE

'Love', is a warm
glowing feeling.
One is floating on air.
But, when you are sad,
and lonely.
Love, lifts you out of
the depths of despair.
Love is a bond between
lovers, promises made above
all others, only they can
share.
Yet, love can grow stale and boring
The beauty it once brought disappears.
Then love turns to sorrow
and heartache.
Love brings bitterness
Hate and tears.

Doreen Petherick Cox

RULES OF ENGAGEMENT

You shall avoid *confrontation*,
And I shall not outstay my welcome
Set out our plan for *retreat*.

I shall not pick unless picking is requested,
Or laugh or complain *unjustly,* or
Even if *justly*, I shall not, to keep the *peace*.

You shall not lose your temper, or if so,
You shall grovel and beg *pardon*, and say you didn't mean it so,
I shall stay *polite,* and *calm*, and not let *emotion* show.
You shall hide your feelings, safely locked away, *protected*.

I shall prop up your ego, if you in return,
Will do the same to mine
And *protect* you from *outside forces,*
The ugliness of the cold *world,*
Set out in stark *black* and *white*.

But our barricaded inside will be colour,
The orange fire glow, greens and blues
Of the *TV set* and the warm yellow
And pinks of the morning sunlight glow.

Structured, *ruled* organised *bliss*
Now we plan our next fifty years
Then spend the next fifty years planning
Escape.

Rebecca Summers

MILLENNIUM

Two moons walked on
An icy lake of stardust drifted by.
A lone star super nova
Then a darkness.
Millenniums of time the light has travelled
To be gone long after the end.
A solar flare touched Venus
The universe to burn.
To all that walked on Jupiter
On Pluto and Mars
Turning, spinning, motion of the night.
Two moons collide
The last whale dies
Ambergris remains.
The synchronicity of life and death
The universe retains.
Two moons walked on
Distant galaxy repeating
All around was moving by.

Alison Clifton

ME AND MY DOG

When I first had my dog he was
fluffy and small, he would run
around and bark at anything he saw.
He would scare off the postman
when he came to our house,
and the poor postman would
creep like a mouse. But now my
dog's much quieter and gracefully
settles down, by a cosy warm
fire and sleeps safe and sound.
And although he's much older and
quiet in many ways, I still love
my dog in his old age.

Elizabeth McFarlane

STAGE FRIGHT

The stage beset me,
trembling with fear I stood
behind the curtain,
waiting to find rapport with an audience.
For the first time
I was to ascertain
what it was like to bare my soul.
Heart and soul went into the verse,
this I can recall
I was upon the stall
as if for sale,
I felt I'd be judged
but I had to do it.
I like a challenge,
it was all fun,
hard work and perspiration,
sheer determination,
my performing was bold
underneath I was cold,
great hilarity stage
I was a *rage*.

Diane Nunnerley

TAKING STOCK

Why do we hate the world so much?
Have we lost the common touch?
It's them or me, it's do or die,
What are all the reasons why?

We all want the illusive ideal
which we know in fact is very unreal.
So make the most of being here
for soon we all will disappear.

What will it be like when I get up there?
When finally shedding my earth borne care.
I'll stand all alone at that pearly white gate
leaving behind all that toil, love and hate.
St Peter will say 'Well never mind lass
I'll just put your name on this heavenly pass.'

I'll meet all my loved ones,
or so I've heard told,
but will they be young or will they be old?
I hope I can run, I like doing that best,
on a soft fluffy cloud I could then take a rest.
But during the meantime I'm calm and controlled,
and not in a hurry, I'll wait till I'm old.

Patricia Bibby

A Mother's Loss

For nine months he snuggled
Inside his mother's womb,
His own little hideaway
His private little room.
How lovingly she stroked him
After every little kick,
And never once did she complain
Although she felt so sick.
And there was such excitement
The day that he was born,
The doctors gathered round him
All looking quite forlorn.
I don't think he will make it
The words cut like a knife,
But we'll do everything we can
To save his tiny life.
All that night they battled
All she could do was pray,
But only two days later
Jesus took his soul away.
His mother's heart was broken
The pain she felt so deep,
She gazed upon his tiny form
Not dead but sound asleep.
We'll have to take him from you now
A kindly doctor said,
And fighting back her pain and grief
She kissed his little head.
The memory of her little boy
Will stay deep in her heart,
She never will forget him
Or the day they had to part.

N D Handley

THE BOY

The boy wanted to love,
He yearned to be loved.
He walked in darkness,
He walked in daylight,
Looking in eagerness and suspicion.
The further he walked,
The more he cried.
The farther he looked,
The less he saw.
It was not until he stumbled and fell,
That he realised,
He could not love another
Until he found love,
In him, for himself.

Gordon Lott

FORGOTTEN GRANDFATHER

He left me when I was young
3-4 I don't know.
I saw him lying there
Awake and well
Or so I thought
Yet, no -
He was ill.
I couldn't tell, everyone acting fine.
Then I never saw him again.
And I asked my parents
Where is he?
But mouths stayed closed
I realised he wasn't around . . .
And now I watch old videos
Tears block up against my eyes
But he is not forgotten
Not a word about him
But he's always on my mind
I hope he hears this
'Cause I miss him
I really miss him.

Stuart Saw (10)

TIME

The clock on my bedside table
is silent during the day.
At night its rhythmic ticking
chases the minutes away.

Cutting them off my life span,
like pearls from a precious chain,
Once lost to infinity
they cannot return again.

How can I capture moments,
and make them mine forever?
By filling the time I have
with pleasure and endeavour.

Lilian Bernard Levi

HALLOWED GROUND

Damp, dark resting place
sleep for those who have suffered
memorial stone.

Flowers placed in a stone vase
thoughts spoken out loud to him
we are missing you.

Dorothy Thornley

CAPITAL PUNISHMENT

There for years serving time,
Left to rot in all that grime.
They don't deserve to be free
and never shall be
But why is it that they still have to be in our society?
Does any one want them? Please can you say,
Or can we give it to them, the price they should pay.
The fear, the hurt, the pain they cause
Surely, it would be cheaper than kept behind doors.
'An eye for an eye,' 'a life for a life,'
A small compensation for all that strife.
Killing has proved to be inhumane
but why shouldn't these criminals be treated the same.
The same as their victims
The families, the friends.
The day will come and soon will be,
the day that killers will never walk free.

Sarah Deacon

A Winter's Day

Falling white flakes
There's ice on the lakes
Ducks sliding everywhere
There must be something under there,
The sky is like a white blanket so soft,
I wonder if I could touch it from the loft.

The houses all look like birthday cakes
Made by tiny little flakes
The snow is falling down, down, down
Swivelling, swerving, round and round.

I'm going out in the cold
My mum has stopped my making moulds,
I've wrapped up warm, hat, coat and scarf
I'm going out to have a laugh.

It's slushy, cold and footprints in the snow
This wintry weather makes my cheeks glow,
I've gone back inside to get warm by the fireside
I'm all nice and warm
Oh look! It's a snow storm.

Suzanna Culshaw

THE FOX

The sly fox curls his bushy tail,
He shrieks then gives a frightened wail,
In the distance he can hear,
The sounds his family lives to fear.

The sound of hooves they pound and pound,
The cry of men, the yell of hounds.
Young ones curl up close to Mum,
The old fox jumps and starts to run.

The chase begins he cannot hide,
No trees, no holes on mountainside.
Nowhere to go, they catch up quick,
The hounds, the horn, it is quite sick.

The head is torn, the hounds are fed
Tail is hung, the ground is bled.
The young ones wait for Dad to call,
But now his head hangs on a wall.

Christine Cocken

GONE AT LAST

    Hurrah!
    She's gone!
That horrible smell, pong,
That horrible voice, screech.
Once a bully,
Always a bully.
She was big,
Gruesome and grotesque.
And I despised her.
Now she's gone,
I've waited 10 years
And that holy terror
Has gone!
    Celebration!
    Hurrah!
That's what I want
    Forever!
But she *is* coming back
    (Double groan!)
    Next Year!

    The Devil has
    Gone!
    Gone!
    Gone!
    Gone!

Laila Street

THOSE MEN (BEF 1940)

Those men were standing on the beach
Looking out to sea,
The Hun with arms outstretched to reach
Those men who would be free.

Those men whose clothing, battle scarred,
Covered hearts still strong,
Those men who'd fought a long rear guard
Still sang their triumph song.

Those men who scanned the channel wide
For any kind of craft,
The dunes the only place to hide
When planes the beaches strafed.

Those men, the ones we left behind,
Those beaches would not see,
Those men to whom fate was unkind,
Had set their comrades free.

Those other men who would not see
The safety of our shores,
For five more years they'd not be free,
But prisoners of war.

Those men who on the beaches stood
Slowly got away,
Back home to loved ones so they could
Fight on another day.

Those men of naval and small ships
Who got us all away,
A prayer of thanks upon our lips
As we our homage pay.

Those men had no counselling
After those days of strife,
Those men just went on soldiering
And carried on with life.

Those men whose war was six years long
In many battle zones,
Can after fifty five years on,
Give thanks for loving homes.

To all those men our nation owes
A debt of priceless cost,
For all these men our nation knows
This peace must not be lost.

Fred Foster

LONDON BLITZ (1940-41)

O'er London Town as twilight gently fades to shadowy dusk
So brightly hangs the moon 'mid a swiftly darkening sky
Footsteps hurrying homeward echo through the quiet streets
And fiercely burning city fires send smoke palls rising high

Through scudding clouds a Hunter's moon illumines all below
From Belgravia's stately mansions to East End terrace home
O'er Thames-side docks low clouds reflect the reddening glow
As London waits expectantly for the ordeal yet to come

Soon sirens wail their mournful songs, a threatening refrain
A warning message wise to heed, of perils night now brings
As distant guns sound closer they herald the menacing drone
Of a myriad roaring engines, bearing death beneath their wings

Searchlights' questing fingers closely search the night-time sky
Seeking out the bombers as through the clouds they fly
Pursued by brilliant shrapnel bursts, they try to lose the lights
Seeking a safer sanctuary in the darkness of the sky

Proud London now surrenders the refuge of dark night
Bright flares fall slowly earthwards, shedding incandescent light
St Paul's great dome revealing, the silver ribbon of the Thames
Lighting all the landscape with a harsh and dazzling light

The target. now lit brightly, the bombs begin their fall
Spawning a myriad angry fires, till all London seems aglow
In garden shelters families meet to survive the fiery storm
Humble folk, little time for fear, stand firm against the foe

Morning comes but slowly, dawn lightens the eastern sky
Rubble strews the battered streets, shattered windows blindly stare
The bombers flee the rising sun, leaving carnage in their wake
Sown are the seeds of a harvest, they too, one day, will share.

Francis Sawyer

A Day To Remember

'D' minus two and so much to be done
Before we sail off to encounter the Hun
A jab from the MO to ward off all ills
Draw ration packs, life jackets, sea-sickness pills.

At Briefing they told us 'Now just get this right'
It's only the Germans that we have to fight'
The French are our friends, so do treat them well
And try to preserve the Entente Cordiale.

As we marched to embark on our moored LCI
Wrens from their bedrooms were waving goodbye
With joy and delight we all turned to stare
Some were in undies, and others quite bare.

The thousands of craft made a wonderful sight
As we headed for France fit and eager to fight
We planned to de-bark feeling ready to kill
But struggled ashore looking green and quite ill.

Though the Navy had promised we wouldn't get damp
We all disappeared as we jumped off the ramp
We paid little heed to machine gun and mortar
As we made for the shore under six feet of water

Like Venus we surfaced, aggressively holding
Our fierce-looking bicycles, infantry, folding.
It must have dismayed the terrified Hun
Who possibly thought them a new type of gun.

We fought through the beach head then counted the cost
To our relief there were very few lost.
The bicycles, too, were checked at this juncture
No damage at all - not even a puncture.

All through the day we continued to fight
Then dug ourselves in at the coming of night.
From the depth of our trenches we gazed at the sky
And dreamed of the Wrens who had waved us goodbye!

Cyril Rand

THE ELYSIAN FIELDS
(Les Champs Elysees)

Beyond these hills,
in beauty behold
the fields of Elysia
gleaming in gold
The fair corn blowing
in the gentle wind,
The daffodils dancing,
with heads held high,
The blue of the cornflowers
as blue as the sky.
The sun shining warm,
to brighten your day,
a place of Paradise,
where one might stay
To dream of happiness and love,
giving thanks for our beautiful earthly home,
till we dwell together in heaven above.

Elisabeth James

A Nice Cup Of Tea

I was but a lad a private in the ACC
Boarding a troop ship bound for the beaches of Normandy
All too soon and at sea we transferred to an LCT
Commands were given once on board
Then suddenly ramps were lowered on a beach named Sword
The beach was crowded, comrades wounded but most were dead
We carried on to achieve our objective which lay ahead
A supplies dump was established and arrayed
An enemy target as their shells displayed
Enemy aircraft were soon overhead
Then all hell broke loose as its bombs were shed
We carried on we did not yield
To a corner of a foreign field
I collected my cooker a hydra burner No 3
There were smiles all round, come on lads it's time for tea
It was expected we were British you see
And everyone knows the British stop everything
For a nice hot cup of 'Rosie Lee' and expected of me
Even in the midst of battle on the beaches of Normandy.

Aubrey Henstock

SOMME AND ON

I sit here in sadness eighty years on,
Thinking of those who died on the plains of the Somme.
I struggle to comprehend why so many young died at once,
The poppies now an epitaph to their final chance.

> Was it sunny then as it is today?
> Did you think of loved ones -
> Did you think to pray?
> When you heard the whistle did you want to go?
> Were the bullets merciful -
> Or did you die slow?

I think of you now as you all fight for that ground,
And the thousands of myself lying dead all round.
More pieces of silver to fill the traitor's purse,
Death rides proud still today to fulfil his curse.

Peter James Warr

SHADOWS

It's evening time for you Big John
Still the morning for John now gone.
Have you filled your given day?
Poor John no more cannot say.
When 'twas dawn for both of you,
Young men in your Air Force blue.
Both shared the time allotted equal
Divided though saw its sequel.
Sent aloft, formation flight
With the future well in sight.
Flying eastward, face the sun.
From whence tomorrow had begun.
Your horizon was so near
Compared with his I sadly fear.
Young men in your Air Force blue,
Now just one where there were two.
Evening now Big John days gone.
For John no more it wasn't long.

Barbara Moore

ARTHUR

I was only two when dad went to war
He proudly belonging to the Tanks Corps
Was blown up in a tank, the desert hot
Poor man beside him was killed on the spot
Blind - he was nursed by nuns in Italy
Year later, Austrian doctor helped him see
The operation was a great success
Transfer German prison camp - what distress
Missing - telegram, mum thought he was dead
Pint of cabbage water - slice of brown bread
Saw lad of seventeen give up and lie
Lad succeeded - he willed himself to die
I nearly eight when this stranger came back
Rough khaki uniform - bulging rucksack.

Jenny Ambrose

SAILOR

He was so young and full of vigour;
Sharp as a knife, he cut a fine figure.
The naval uniform made the fine male,
So full of pride he set off to sail.
To sea he went; battles to fight,
All through the day - all through the night.
Thrice he was torpedoed, thrice he survived,
The inscrutable grip that the sea did provide.
A watery grave that he did escape,
Only to find a disabled body was encased -
In plaster for a year. But he returned.
By the grace of God - although infirm,
He returned to his wife and children so serene,
Grateful for his life after serving his King.

Valerie Marshall

THE GULF WAR

. . . Grief in my heart -

Summer and sun,
Sand and heat,
Acetone and sweat,
Gripes at my soul -
No sound in the sand.

They are sleeping.
Run scorpion, run!
Fly carrion, fly!
My ears are deaf.
My eyes are blind.
No-one stirs on the ground -
No cries, no sound.
The desert of blast
With whistling scuds -
Now ghosts. We joke
At *death* from chemical war.

I live. Most are dead.
Shadowy friends -
They journey to sunset.
They sleep. I wake.
I'll avenge their death.
God will surmount!

Move to your sounds!
You will be smote
By mites of smoke.
I laugh at you, *death.*
You strangle my breath.
I am safe, glorious peace.
I am safe save for grief.
Tanks pattern the sand -
A desertless strand.

Nola B Small

REMEMBRANCE SUNDAY

On the eleventh hour,
of the eleventh day,
of the eleventh month,
Just stop what you are doing
Spare two minutes of your life,
to think of those who gave their life,
for you and all other defenceless
men, women and children
around this world
who have relied upon our soldiers brave,
in their times of trouble.
Do not let their memory,
fade and die.
Of brave, young men and women
of past conflicts far and wide.
Just wear your poppy and be humble
it is not for the world to see,
but for you to give thanks,
to the dead and disabled servicemen,
of this, our land.
To show that you do care.
On Remembrance day
as the poppies fall
to shed a tear, you will,
do not be ashamed
just be grateful that you,
can live *your* life to, the full.

Lynda Banks

ONE OF THE FEW

Don't pass me by without a care
For I am still around somewhere
High in the sky above the cloud
I'm up here with the rest of my crowd
A crowd of men so fair and brave
Who gave their all so Britain could be saved
And as I lie beneath the soil
I can say I've done my toil.

Marianne G Sutherland

CHARLIE

I knew a man in Air Force blue,
His name was Sergeant Charlie Drew,
A better man you never knew,
A pilot of great renown,
And very handy, to have around,
He never got worried, or flustered at all,
Especially if a 109 got him in a stall,
He'd bank and turn,
And loop and roll,
He'd shout 'Climb up,
I'll have a go,'
He'd then take him out
The danger he drew,
That very brave man,
In Air Force blue.

Pip 'C'

Requiem

Under age so many lied
Answering Kitchener's rallying pride.
Comrades all received the King's shilling
Journeyed far to fields of killing.
Assailed by constant screaming shells
So unlike England's village bells.
Home thoughts flashed through minds in turmoil
Manning trenches on foreign soil.
Foolish orders from the top
Caused so many hearts to stop.
Over the top and into hell
Hoping to dodge transgressor's shell.
Soldiers soldiers all around
Fell like snowflakes to the ground.
Patriotic strong and bold
Lying rigid still and cold.
Minor gains for major losses
Such a waste for nation's bosses.
Conflagration so rarely seen
Became reality in nineteen fourteen.
Generals hailed a welcome peace
Regiments wept for their deceased.
Returning home with hope and glory
A hero's land another story.
Blood red poppies in profusion
Cover landscapes of retribution.
Reminder still of those who lie
Beneath an ever-changing sky.

Arthur Pugh

THE FORGIVING FIELD

And in the dawn of screaming hush
Before the monumental climb,
The Sunday spires call back their sons
And whisper through the parting hope
That God will guide the steely blade
Whose solid stock lies still for now.

A Colonel, rising from the warmth of bed
Says all is well, just one last push
Before we see the cheerful, choppy channel
Which leads to those cathedral bells
And lanes of leafy light with five-bar gates
Into the fields of green where ne'er a trench
Has ever been a heartless home.

Then once again, the whistle's shrill
Says up and over, lads,
See now the mud of sudden death
As those who shared your deadly fear,
Face forward, say their last goodbye.

And when before you, arms aloft,
The sorry eyes are slowly raised,
They ask, amid the howling rain
To see forgiveness in a face
Whose vision in this day of death
Has been dear friends of faded life.
And yet those eyes plead long to show
A sorrow that so slowly grows
Till tears fall freely to the ground
And arms embrace in single mind.

Roy Williams

OUR FINEST HOUR

A single Spitfire in the sky
Was omen that a war was nigh.
With Hitler sitting on the fence
In 'Thirty-nine' the air was tense.

The Nazi power was soon let loose,
With trumped-up charges as excuse
To launch a Blitzkrieg on our land,
'Gainst which perforce we made a stand.

Soon streets were dark as lights went out
In case the Germans were about;
The able-bodied took up arms,
And those at home endured alarms.

Caught unawares and ill-prepared,
To beat the Hun we nigh despaired.
But at their posts 'Dad's Army' stood
Though lightly armed, 'gainst Hitler's brood.

Then brave young airmen saved the day
Till bombers nightly went their way
To rain destruction on the foe,
And smash his factories down below.

As war developed things got worse
And air-raids soon became a curse.
Our seamen, who had left their wives
To man the convoys, risked their lives.

And air-raid wardens, firemen too;
All played their part . . . and so did you!
With tightened belts and rations small
The Nation rallied to the Call.

We pulled our weight against the foe;
'Our finest hour' . . . was it not so?

Lionel Reid

PIPE DREAMS

Birds fly in the air.
Angels sing, flowers bloom, and the world
is at ease once more.

How long will that last?
Next time we want another man's land
will men again make war?

We have not yet learned
how to live in harmony and peace
by the world's natural laws.

The animals who roam free
are better than us, they don't torture
or break down other people's doors.

If we could only be
like them, we would all roam free,
living by that mystical lore.

Then planet earth might be
saved from destruction, and there would be
hope for our children.

Daf Richards

COUNTING THE COST

A soldier, and I did my best
Went into battle with the rest
Prepared to fight, prepared to die
And didn't count the cost.

We trained for war, that was our task,
And with the call we did not ask
Why we should have to go.
We'd had our day, and earned our pay
And didn't count the cost.

So, in the battle there I fell
We all fought hard, we all fought well.
I surely didn't want to die,
But never thought to ask once why
I had to pay the cost.

My mother grieves, as mothers do,
And there are many others who
Will shed a quiet tear and sigh
For their own sons who had to die.
They still must pay the cost.

So, as my body lies at rest
Accountants now take up the list,
This is when they must be active
To make the next war cost effective
Oh, they will count the cost.

And so you lads who follow me
I wish you self-same victory
And hope you triumph in your war
That there should be a budget for
So you can count the cost.

Robert A Plummer

GHOSTS OF NINETEEN FORTY

Squadron upon squadron
With glint of hallowed glow
In mid-day heat of August
Huge Armada flying low.

The fallen at the zenith
of a quality of Men
Produced by old democracy
When one the worth of ten.

The intervening years, till now
Each one towards decline
Of the substance of those airmen
Alone to front the line.

I look above a field in Kent
One place unchanged by time
My vision crowds with aircraft
That swoop, spiral and climb.

The ghosts of battles' pilots
Remain as witness to
Destruction of a way of life
Bequeathed by they - *the few!*

Henry J Green

STOLEN YOUTH

That laughing smile that forever is gone,
those sparkling eyes not there.
They're just pools of molten madness,
surrounded by an expression of deep despair.
His years of youth were stolen,
in the shifting desert sand.
When he was struck down by a sniper's bullet,
far from his native land.

Strange people come and see him,
and they call him by a name.
He is indifferent to whom they are,
everyone looks the same.
The woman keeps crying and she calls him son,
but she has a stranger's face.
Although there is something familiar
               when she holds him close,
In her soft and warm embrace.

They called him a hero, though he knew not why,
strange men shook him by the hand.
They pinned a medal on his chest,
and said he was a credit to his land.
The strange men soon forgot him,
although they wished him well.
They are looking for some other sons,
to send to an insane hell.

David Galvin

THE HIGHWAYMAN

I am too absorbed for
The telling tick-tock
Of Time and clock
Pilfering precious moments
With no thought or guile?
Ensnared by each instant
He turns over the chapters of my life
Before I am braced
To face and see
What will there be?

My infant is born.
I stroke her silent skin
Caress her calmness
Claim her close;
Hankering for the halt
Of the candour of the clock
The indifference of passing hours,
The years that will rob me of her.

Is Time innocent
In tip-toeing away
With what is so priceless.
Or is he a highwayman
In disguise, premeditating
Our lives and our demise?

Michele Glazer

INFORMATION

We hope you have enjoyed reading this book - and that you will continue to enjoy it in the coming years.

If you like reading and writing poetry drop us a line, or give us a call, and we'll send you a free information pack.

Write to :-

**Arrival Press Information
1-2 Wainman Road
Woodston
Peterborough
PE2 7BU**